HEART
OF
GOLD

WITH SILVER FLAMES

CHERYL KNOLL

Printed in the United States of America

ISBN 979-8-89114-224-4 (sc)
ISBN 979-8-89114-225-1 (hc)
ISBN 979-8-89114-226-8 (e)

Library of Congress Preassigned Control Number: 2025918517

2025.11.17

MainSpring Books
5901 W. Century Blvd
Suite 750
Los Angeles, CA, US, 90045

www.mainspringbooks.com

Contents

Our Heart

Our heart of gold with silver flames
Engraved in love, it bares our names
A gift from our Divine
Our hearts beat as one
I am your moonlight
You are my sun
There is no distance in love heart to heart
Remember this when we are apart
I watched a flame engrave our names
Our heart then breathed with silver flames
We were chosen to share one soul
Our heart of gold now makes us whole
It is the purest love that hearts will mesh
To shine as gold, though they are flesh
Hold me with your body close to mine
I want to feel the silver flames
Of love that shine

New World Light

The awakened are ever evolving
They still feel earth
Even though they leave the world behind
They will shine higher frequencies
As they shed the world
They will shine a new light on the world
They are a beacon of light for searching eyes
To see, to find, to feel and hold the light themselves
They will be in the world
Not of it
But only as a new light

Meditating

I fade away
I cannot feel the outline of my body
Chantress Seba blesses my soul as I listen
The hand pan music falls as raindrops on my soul
In her ancient temple meditation music, I am myself
When I listen, I also feel you
What a mystical form of music that I can feel you
I am myself with you
Without you I would only be self
With you, I am myself
Whole

His Breath, My Life

In the stillness of the night
I hear his breath
The breath from his body moves my soul
It reaches my heart
The breath of the man I love
It is the breath that gives life to my living
The breath that powers everything I love about him
His body, his strength, his mind
His humor
I reach over and place my hand on his heart
I reach over and softly kiss his lips
Breath to breath
He responds
With his well-intentioned love

Stand With Me

I stand in the light sure footed
Leaving the darkness of shadows behind
Illuminated with love in this light
It is not a mysterious light
It is the light of love
Step into love's light and stand with me
The light will reveal we were two halves
Two halves stepping out of their shadows
To become one whole being
Shadows belong to the darkness
Live in the light of love with me

On My Mind

I sat on raindrops on a chair
I felt your presence everywhere
The fireflies sparkled brightly that night
I felt you in the firefly's light
Every firefly light that sparkled to see
Sent messages of your love for me
I gazed into a star filled sky
Wondering if you felt me nearby
I focused on that star as you
Wondering if you miss me too
It has only been two weeks of days
I find myself missing you
In so many ways
The "me" inside, I hide from the world
Your deep love leaves my heart unfurled
Raindrops and fireflies are special in kind
Like the way you appear on my mind
Like the night sky full of stars to see
I know there is only one star for me
I thought it was mysterious why I dwell on you
When love is destined, its light shines through
In the moments it sparkles like fireflies
Each new sparkle brings a surprise
The beaming star I chose to see
Was you giving your love to me

Does He See Me?

If he could only see me
He would see love in human form
His eyes look at me
And I wonder
Does he see me?
Does he see me, who I am?
If he only knew my feelings of love
My love is for him
Unconditional love meant only for him
I asked God and his universe for help
How do I help him see me?
My angels intervened with messages
You cannot help him
He needs to help himself
What you desire, desires you
Love yourself first
Stay patient and wait for divine timing
P.S., he loves you, and he is in pain
It is a man thing, he needs time

I Like You

You can be yourself with me
I will be myself with you
Though we share the same soul
We can walk apart as two
And still be one
I do not want to take away from you
I would take your love but
There is no need to take it
You give it to me freely
You are generous with your love for me
Be yourself with me
You
I like you
I love you

Mystical Silence

We have been told, silence is golden
And it is, though more than golden
Silence is mystical
When love is pulsing with blood
Rushing through the heart
When there is a silence and he fills it
With his presence in my body
When I feel him and he is not here
He is
In this golden mystical silence
He is here
He is coming in golden
Silently loud and strong

His Treasure

He found his treasure

He loved her with unbridled passion

She was the reason he was alone for so many years

He did not know her yet

Not until now and there would be no other woman

Who could fill the role she would play

Though it was no role

She was real and in real form

His love in the form of a woman

The woman meant to be his

She would not be playing him

Or toying with his affection

She also waited her whole life for him

Love is not meant for all to find at a youthful age

Some loves age like the finest of wines

He found her

See how his masculinity shines in her presence?

He would care for her every need

She would love him for that

He would love her with an unwavering love
She returned it ten-fold
Suffer his wrath if you disrespect her
She would be everything he ever wanted
Or needed
Let other women be jealous
Try to replace her or find his favor
That would be their mistake
His eyes will only ever see her
His treasure

Where He Is

Be baptized
In the birds singing
In the cloud cover
In the wildlife traveling through
In the trees
Be baptized in admiration when
They are swaying in the breeze
Make your covenant with nature
How could it not be yours
God created it
Let your prayers be heartfelt
In the white sand and blue waters
In the leaves that change with the season
Let their beauty fill you with awe
Worship in the glistening, glittering snow
Watch the snow falling heavy and let stillness prevail
Thank God for the billions of stars in a night sky
My church is God's universe
My soul worships him everywhere he is
The soul always knows it belongs
Where He is

He Loves Me

He is a reservoir of sacred love for me
His love is divine
When the world adds weight to my being
I search for him
I find comfort in the arms that hold me
I will be the only one to know his love
My divine masculine and his divine love
Are for me, his divine feminine
He cherishes me
He cares for my every need
He loves me...he loves me
He loves me
He takes the world out of my mind
Welcome to my world

The Love Game

I lost myself in the awakening of love

My mind and heart felt captive

As if bound in chains

Life stopped for me

I fell into a trap of waiting to receive love from him

It was not the time for him to give it

My canvas stayed blank

No colorful words from him

No reaching out that I longed for

Only to question if this was a cruel trick

I was not seeking love

It found me

It is his turn Lord

Do the same to him while I wait

My mind is now free of his power

And again, my soul has control

I will have sympathy for him Lord

When it happens to him

Then I will love him

Your Voice Sonnet

My heart stirs as I hear you say my name
The voice that speaks it moves inside my soul
My soul's awareness responds to your voice
Soul to soul recognition, we are one

You call my name, and I know what you need
I come to you and here I am for you
Body, mind and soul, I give you my love
You return love as only you can do

Say my name with soft breath while we share love
Your voice, the only voice my heart will hear

Warmest Love

Like the sun we rise again
To find our way to shine our light
To give what we can to the day
To shine inside when it is night
We do our best to shine through clouds
Taking our place after rain
We give our warmth to hurting souls
We do our part to ease their pain
Love so powerful as the sun
Is what we give to live each day
Occasionally two suns will join
Together we rise
Together we lay

Feeling Our Words

When you feel a whole vocabulary in your being
There are words that you desire to express
Though they will not form into sound
Expression may need to take place with bodies
What I desire to say wants to be expressed with my body
You are not expressing your feelings with words also
I know you feel what I feel
We feel it but cannot verbalize it
Express yourself to me and I will reciprocate
After we express ourselves with our bodies
We will express ourselves with soft words

I Found Her

For years I sought her
I imagined her
Who she is
Where she is
I knew she would radiate with love
That I knew
I knew she would be a woman with love
Life, people, jobs, circumstances
All kept her from finding her way
All the searching
Endless waiting for love
Led me to her
I found her
In the mirror

Eternal Love

Love transcends our earthly realm
It lives eternally for some
Rare souls that live and know love's power
Will find each other again in time
True love will seek and search its own
Always feeling a sense of missing
Till it finds its other half again
My love will find your love again
When your love is searching for mine

I Love Heavy Words

His words are few though they carry weight
His words are treasures when we date
His voice is healing to my ears
His tone erases inner fears
He speaks to me, straight to my heart
Some words cemented, not to part
His words speak love and calm my soul
I enjoy giving him control
I love him Lord
I will forever
To be without his voice
Please, never
He is not the only one with words to say
I tease him with love
With words that stay
My vocabulary knows how to play with tone
When I give him my love, with words for his own

At times, our words will lead to bed
Where words give way to love instead
That is where cherished words are said
Heavy words for the heart and head
They carry weight
They carry weight, though few
The words that fill me
I love you
I love you

Chocolate Love

My strong man has sweet love for me
When he sees chocolate
He will think of me
He knows how much I will thank him
For his thoughtfulness
I will thank him
With love as sweet
He will remember that
The next time he sees chocolate

His "Feelings"

He did not want "feelings" anymore
Just for that, God had opened a door
With pleasure, God pushed him out for fun
You will sure have "feelings" when you are done

She loved you but you were often curt
You ignored her, you know that had to hurt
You liked pretending that she was not there
You looked through her like she was air
You gave attention to other women around
But her, you walked on her like ground
You used to hug her and hold her tight
But you got scared, your "feelings" took flight

She and her love decided to go
You will" feel" her absence and now you know
You will "feel" the most pain you could "feel"
You lost her love, and it was real
The love she takes back will leave a hole
A gaping wound and pain to control
Her love was deep, and you finally "feel"
What it is like to lose a love so real

Your friends just seem to fall away
Your work suffers, so does your play
Other women do not bring you joy
You are a man and now cry like a boy
You want to be alone so you can "feel"
Her presence and her love that was real
You do not know how you will move on
Without her in your life, she is gone
You know you will keep losing sleep
If you cannot get her back to keep

There is only one way to end this mess
It is time for "feelings" you must confess
Find her now and tell her how you "feel"
She will still love you, her love is real

Surender with Forgiveness

In arguments, one side wants the victory sweet

When one side pushes forward with no retreat

When airing a grievance to take a stand

My surrender I offer, love's upper hand

This is love I desire to keep

My ego does not battle; I let it sleep

Forgiveness is the weapon for me

I surrender to set a grievance free

When we mutually forgive and souls emerge

Passions flair, desires surge

Forgiveness is my weapon of choice

I surrender, with forgiveness

To hear love's voice

Mystical Silence

If there is silence between us
We are quiet in love
No constant validating or excessive words
Love is present without words
In the silence I will think of him
I will speak to him with my spirit
He can feel the soul language
I feel it from him also
Our silence is mystical
It is a rare gift for the soul
Invisible, though felt
Felt with our love

Soul Light

Shine your light for me that I may see others
Shine for others that they may see me
Shine your light on me to warm my heart
That it does not become cold
Shine your light on me that I may grow in it
And that I grow more light to shine
My soul glows in this inner light
Soul light reflects love
Soul light is love

The Force

Love is a force of nature
It will sweep across you
Like wind on a barren landscape
Love is like the sun rising
Nothing can stop its destined rising
It can have the force of a raging river
When threatened with loss
Yet it is as gentle as soft rain
And as subtle as a gentle breeze that brings relief
When love meets love
It is a force of the universe
Do not war with this force
Join forces

In the Darkness

Darkness hovered above me as I lay in my bed
I pretended the darkness was a night sky
Though the darkness hovered
I fancied it was full of lights like stars
I could feel the light
In the darkness, I could see the light
The light will shine and guide me
With love
The light will let darkness have no place

Hidden Doorway

I found the hidden doorway found by few
Beliefs fell off as I went through
With trepidation my feet still moved on
To shed myself of me till I was gone
My soul emerged as me upon this path
I found my love and left behind all wrath
The door shut as I left others behind
I found my soul and quieted my mind
As I ascend the stairs I see above
With every step I take
There is more love
The door disappeared that I left behind
It was only meant for me
For me to find

Flowers? Thank You

Should you choose to bring me flowers
You should know I will respond
With soft words of my love for you
With gratefulness, and kissing too
My arms will reach to hold you tight
I will thank you in my way, later tonight
I will make sure I thank you right
Should you choose to bring me flowers
You should know
I will respond

Good Night

The heaviness of the night sets in
It is time for my conscious to travel
To that mystical unconscious
My hands reach to feel your body
My affection and my love search
For your lips to kiss goodnight
Soft words in my mouth search
For your ears
I want to feel the warmth of your embrace
I want to fall asleep full of your love
When my conscious seeps to the unconscious
I want to be full of your love
I will keep it with me as I sleep
It will guide me back to you
To be in love with you again

The "Missing Clouds"

Today, the clouds are hiding the sun
As I think of you, my only one
I stare out the window, coffee in hand
Thoughts of our love
The lay of "our" land
My one and only, I love only you
What I know for sure, I am on your mind too
I can feel you even when you are away
Your mind, your love, the words you say
The way you see me
The way you stare
The way you pull me close when you care
Though you are away
I know you are mine
"Missing you" clouds pass
Your love, for me will shine

Sitting With God

I sit in my gift, in silence
In a quiet house
Sitting in the presence of the Lord
With angels tending
An occasional tone from a wind chime
Is a church bell for my soul
To rest in completeness
And know I am whole
Yes, my ears are ringing
With God's frequency 963 hertz
Brought by a higher dimension
Silence filled with God's gifts
Too numerous to mention
It is God's frequency
I can live with that sound
As I sit in my reverence for God
I sit on holy ground

Love Cards

Playing morning solitaire
I felt his hand caress my hair
He stood close and smelled divine
Every part of him is mine
How quickly he controls my senses
With him I never have defenses
When love arises
We give time for expressing
The cards can wait
When love needs addressing
Today is a day with nothing else pressing
Thank you, my love, for feeling my hair
Do it anytime when you care
Loving you is always in the cards for me
King and queen of hearts
Forever and ever, we will ever be

I Will Be Moonlight

The sun can shine
I will walk as moonlight beneath it
With a glow, I will emanate a soft light
I do not need all of me to show
Though I may occasionally cast a moonbeam
I will shine light in the darkness
Enough for the darkness to give way
I will repel the darkness
It will not be part of me
I do not need to shine brightly
That is not my way
I will walk as glowing moonlight
Where my light lands
It will stay

When Life Gives You Rocks

When you find life gives you obstacles
Rocks so huge they are burdens
Find a crevice in the rock and plant yourself
You see plants and flowers growing in crevices
You be the tree
Plant yourself in a crevice
You can be the tree that proves to the rock
It cannot stop you from living
You will grow despite the rock
Others will look at you with wonderment
How can that be? A tree growing out of a rock
You proved the rock cannot stop you
The plants and flowers growing out of their crevices
Will look up to you

The Power of Love

His love is as intoxicating as wine

His love feels deep

And it is sweet

I am under his influence

When he looks into my eyes

With a look

It is love though there is a wildness to it

Then weak am I

As having too much wine

He can overpower me

With his glance

And I let him

I love his wine

Love Garden

Love gives a peaceful power to the holder of it
Peaceful as a garden tended
Powerful as the one who tends it
Fears cannot overtake like weeds
The tender will speedily remove them
Doubts cannot take root in love
Doubts will be un-watered seeds that cannot grow
Only love will flourish in love's well-tended garden
Love's garden will grow to produce fruits
Fruits of patience, kindness, devotion, and respect
I grew in the power of love
I grew into the power of love
The love I grow and hold
I will give it to you

Thank You Powers

I am grateful to the powers that be
The powers that brought your love to me
Destiny and fate planted my name in your heart
They knew when we met, an awakening would start
They planted your name also
In my heart and my being
To awaken my soul and let love do the seeing
The powers that knew when I heard your tone
That was the frequency my heart would own
I give my love to the powers that be
They let my love find you
They let your love find me

Wolf Heart

He is like a wolf
To my heart, my soul, my love
A wolf will mate for life with his mate
He will stay close and care for her
He does not wander
He does not stray
Regardless of how many she wolves he encounters
They are just she wolves
He is mine for life
And he knows I am his

Strolling

I walked out of the beating sun
To stroll through the trees
For relief
I dissolve in their shade
I feel lightened
My form disappears in this relief
And I feel weightless
Though grounded
You come to my mind
That is how you make me feel

He Out loved Me
(Or Did He?)

I had love to give him
Unconditional, deep, and pure
Amazing heartfelt love
Then he gave me his love
My love paled in comparison
He gave me love that caused my body to ache
Without him
He gave me love that warmed me
Without covers
He gave me love that altered my appearance
I glowed in his love
He gave me abundant love
His love will make my love grow stronger
It was my love though
That made him love me more

Anchor Yourself

Anchor yourself in your soul's presence
Here is your rightful place to stand in stillness
And radiate love as a lighthouse radiates light
Stillness is a heart of gold
Full of love that burns with flames of silver
Purified silver with no imperfections
Awareness fills me
With an overwhelming receptiveness
To a higher power, divine in nature
It is God
Be still and know the power
Live in your soul presence
Anchor yourself in love

I Feel Me

I always knew you
I was always aware of you
Hidden inside of my soul
From the time we signed a soul contract
In another time
Destiny is the gate keeper for time
Destiny awakened you in me
I felt you
I feel you
Wherever time is I feel you
Now I feel me
Now that I feel you
I feel me

Writing Love

I could fill pages with words
And I do
To let you know how much I love you
Though I would prefer
To fill my arms with you
I would prefer
To fill you with feelings
Feelings of my love
Feelings, not words
I would fill you with feelings of my love
To last longer than words on paper
After that
I will fill my words with feelings
And I will fill pages with words

Invisible Presence

Today, I see the birds
Though I really do not see them
Though they are in my sight
I only see you
I see your essence
I feel your presence
I feel as though I am under the influence
Invisible narcotics
Only I am not
Only love can do this to a living soul
I have things I could do
Though I am sitting still in a chair
Seeing birds, though not seeing
I do not want to leave you
Not yet

Living

I transcend the body
Whose feet walk upon the earth
I found love
So great, so deep
An awakening akin to rebirth
Materialism and practices
Others strive for
They are of no interest to me
Now, there is nothing worldly
To hold me to the body
My only want is for love
To radiate and live
Now I live in love so great
My love now
I must give

I Need Help

Could I ever stand in front of him
And not want to put my hands on him
Though his masculinity and magnetism
Could cause me to feel needy
I am not needy
When we stand two feet apart
Or one even
When he puts his face inches from mine
To tell me something in a teasing manner
I try to keep my composure
With dazed eyes and a half smile
Though every cell in my body tells me
Reach out to him
Put my hands on his chest
Feel his biceps
Stand on my toes and try to kiss him
On the outside, my eyes stare
My insides scream
Help me Lord, please
Cause something to happen
Before I embarrass myself

Hanna

She lives in her love
Glowing white gold surrounds her
The purest of gold outlines her being
It is love she radiates
Where she goes
Her love glows
Rare is she
As the rarest, purest gold
Reach out to her
She will give you love
Behold
She will give you the rarest, purest love
To hold

Lessons

I reflect upon the lessons I learned
To find life is not always kind
To feel the deepest love in my soul
Then question, was it just my mind?
Some lessons were painful, harsh at best
Sleepless nights, no sleep, no rest
People come and people go
Some worth knowing
Some not to know
Over giving, do not do
It only makes a lesser you
Give your love to yourself first
Then share it when it grows to burst
Lessons hurt, you may plead no
Lessons cause more love to grow
The love you feel deep in your soul
It is yours to keep
It makes you whole

In Stillness

In stillness I am
In the spring, when I see my first robin
When I see birds return and search
For the earth's offerings to build nests
Spring rains and newly emerging buds
Bring life once more to dormancy

In stillness I am
With a soft breeze on a summer day
While I watch the birds eat from their feeders
They flit and flitter from branch to branch
And the birdbaths become a party

In stillness I am
On a chilly autumn day
Fall leaves turn glorious colors and drift
To the ground
And autumn naps give comfort to the weary

In stillness on a winter day
While snow falls so beautifully
My soul feels like the snow
I embrace the stillness with love
I find myself feeling the love of stillness

In stillness I am

Creation's Secret

The mountains stood in reverence to God in their altitude
To communicate with nature's secret voice
The hills then praised the mountains for their majesty
Preceding the mountains, creation's choice
The meadows thanked the hills for their protection
Beholden to the hills for being there
The water blessed the meadows for their fruitfulness
By providing water for the meadows care
The rocks cried out "Glory to the highest"
In unison with creation, I do the same
With all of life's trials, I am left standing
Undefeated, my soul won the game
I, in unison with creation
Give reverence to the universe so vast
I proclaim with everlasting gratefulness
I know myself
I know true love at last

A Tough Journey

Life can be like living on top of a hill
With a long steep winding road to get there
And some of those steps are painful
When you get to the top, you are there
You are home
And in the back yard is another hill
And you climb it for fun
At the top of the hill is a rock formation
That one you choose not to climb
You just look up at it with awe
It is one huge solid rock
You tell the rock you are already standing
On the greatest solid rock
But someday, you may climb the rock in the back yard
Just for fun

You Were with Me

No matter how far away I traveled
I did not travel away from you
What you are in me
Who you are in me, cannot leave
Miles cannot separate us
Bonded hearts and souls cannot separate
When bonded with love
Unconditional love
It is unbreakable
Miles are only an illusion

Tree Love

I walked along a row of trees

Walking under a row of arching branches

You were waiting at the end

Patiently waiting for me

The shade of the trees felt like the shade of your love

The way your love covers me

And protects me

The trees are strong and tall

As are you

I look up to you with reverence

Just as the branches reach out

Your hand reaches out to me

With curiosity I wonder

Do trees mate?

Where do the little trees come from

We should mate

Prisoner of Love

My heart whispered to my soul
What am I feeling?
The first time I saw you
My mind engaged my soul in an investigation
Was there a transgression?
My heart was free and now it is held captive
For questioning
What was my charge?
Am I guilty of the law of attraction?
My heart was on trial
The jury was my mind and my soul
God, his universe, and my angels
All weighed the matter
Guilty of love
The jury unanimously charged me
Now I am a prisoner of love
I pray for a life sentence

Love Confession

I close my eyes and think of you
I dissolve and become one with the universe
I have no boundaries now
I am wide open with you on my mind

Your love is my sky
My soul has expanded
With love too powerful for me to hold
No boundaries can contain this love
Though my heart makes attempts to tame it
I tend to let this love run wild and free
Though, my love only runs to one
You

Same Soul

Her imagination soared to new heights
The sun was behind her, but she could see
A different sun shining through to her eyes
With her eyelids closed
Waves of inexplicable peace filled every cell
And she disappeared from reality
Her consciousness makes her aware
He is ever present
He may fade from present thoughts
But he lingers in the background
More so loitering
She had to constantly use her soul police
To stop and confront her mind for thinking of him
We let him go
Though he will not go
She saw the invisible hand
Holding and offering a gift
He could see it also
It was not imagination
It was the soul of both
Two halves of the same soul
Cannot rest again
Till they are one

Melt My Heart

Who could melt the ice in my heart?
Only you
Your love burned like fire for me
Your love thawed my frozen heart
Ice melted and flowed as tears
Ice melted and washed away pain
And fear, I passed the fear away in its melting
As my heart warmed, it began to burn also
With passion
Reciprocating the burning love, you gave to me
Love that burns so strongly
Only for each other
My heart would be ice for any other
This love has melted our hearts together
Soldered together with love

Dear Moonlight

Grand rising dear moonlight
You rise and shed light on my love
He is the one I love
With white sheer curtains on open windows
Moving in the breeze
You cast soft light on my lover
As we lay in our bed
He is not only visible in your light
He is visible in every way to me
I see his strength
I see his softness, not seen by others
I see his heart, his soul, his love
He shows all of himself to me
I see him
I see love in human form
And dear moonlight
He is handsome in your light

Love Breeze

As the flowers bounce on summer days
The tricky breeze and how it plays
My thoughts and feelings turn to you
I love you through and through
And through
Your love, my breeze
Not to resist
Your love blooms when you are missed
You tease me like a summer breeze
My love feels you
Come love me please

I Am

I do not hide my feelings and words
Nor do I have to expose my feelings or words
My feelings though deep and suppressed
May occasionally appear on my surface
To share with others who see and feel
My words are only thoughts expressed
Should I desire to share my thoughts
These thoughts I will share
Everything God gave me
I am
Everything God is in me
I am
I am overflowing with gratefulness
For God and His universe
He created my soul
I am my soul
I am

Translation

My heart is deciphering a language
Distantly familiar
My soul helps my heart to translate
Slowly, the language becomes fluent
It brings life to feelings
Now the feelings translate into words
Words the heart can understand
It is love speaking
My heart replies to this love
I feel love
I can love
And I love you

Fortress of Love

When evening falls and I am with you
You are a fortress of love for me
You are strong and I do not need to be
Your love is like a guardian for me
To watch over me and protect me
And I love that
You keep a mental check list
You see to all my needs
It is your nature to care for the one you love
I am fortunate to be your recipient
When God gave you to me to love
When God gave me to you to love
It was his divine plan
You are my fortress of love

After the Fire

Trees lay burned, bare of branches on the mountain side
The forest trees, as strong as they were
Succumbed to a greater force
After the devastation, and the passing of time
New life will come
In time, new life will grow
So are we, like trees
It can happen even to the strongest
Not only fire, but death, disease
Lost or unreciprocated love
In time, new life will come
You will recover and a new life will appear
The burned logs can lay as memories
Someday, you will want to remove your burned logs
To make way for your new life

Walk Softly in Love

To awaken love prematurely is akin
To walking through tall grass
And startling a spotted fawn
It runs away
The frightened fawn runs
Though you know it did not run far away
It sought protection
The same as when a heart runs to feel safe
The fawn and the heart
Both are afraid of the unknown
The fawn will seek protection from its mother
The heart will remember the feeling
It will want to sooth the fear
And it will want more love

Double Vision

He was running with a mirror before him
He was running from love
He ran with intensity
In the mirror before him, he could see her reflection
He did not realize he was not only running from her
But also, to her
She was there in his background behind him
She was also in the mirror before him
What he was running from, he was also running to
She had compassion for him, his uneasy state
She turned around, the vision of her now a blur
He was running from himself, not her
No reflection of her in his mirror
He now saw his soul much clearer
Her energy gone, he found he was missing
Her lips untouched, he wished he were kissing
Chaos was his state of mind
She drove him crazy, he would find
In the mirror only his reflection was found
He stopped running to turn around
She was there
She was holding space for him
She was not going anywhere

Running is a state of mind
He was there; with his soul to find
He found his soul and hers as well
Running was a living hell
He vowed never again to run
(Well maybe a little)
Just to let her catch him
For fun

I See You

I will see you in the morning light
I see the man you are
I see you in the evening light
I see you in your fullness
I see you in the moonlight
I see you with love
I not only see you
I know you
With my love

The Awakening Kiss

Our lips touched to share a kiss
My new world opened after this
My heart opened and swallowed me whole
I re-emerged now, as my soul
Deep is love when it is real
So deep, there is no past to heal
It goes away, so far away
Now, only love can stay
Only room for love to grow
With this glowing energy, the soul will know
Love so deep, the kiss our seal
When a soul feels love
The love is real

Snow, Love, You

This snow falls with a sacredness
Falling as though it were love
My human form transcends to the spiritual
My soul, enveloped with love in this beauty
Adds wholeness to my peace
To be in love with you manifests this feeling
Your love warms me
My heart is a hearth with flames of love
Flaring with desire for your love
My love for you is as pure as the snow
I have love for you
My heart is sending you a message
See me soon
Let my love fall softly and purely
Over you

Become Love

When you are capable of embodying love
You will belong to the universe
You will be one with all there is
Wholeness will be your virtue
To be whole, and to be filled with love
You will find that you have found
What all others are searching for

Vines That Bind Sonnet

Intertwined in love, heart vines are braided
Though in two bodies, our hearts beat as one
With vines of virtue braided to stay strong
Cords not to break, powerful as the sun

Should the sun not shine on the outer side
Know it shines with love, my heart to your heart
Should the clouds cover us, they are fleeting
The vines of love will hold; they will not part

Love to love the vines grow to ever twine
My love is ever your love, yours is mine

Soul Living

Here in this peaceful silence, I am my soul
My body is invisible for now
My mind takes a passive roll as
My soul tells my mind to behave itself
Soul control over mind control
My soul lives in peace of fullness
My soul is but a traveler in time
A recipient of divine timing and destiny
Your soul is my destiny
My soul is receptive to you
To your soul and your love
Speaking of love…
In this peaceful silence
My body desires to express myself and
My mind tires of taming and would like to run wild
I am receptive to only you
Do you feel receptive?
We should make love
I have soul love for you

Everlasting Love

Life is a gift for living
Dying is a gift for returning to love
Returning to the source of love
The source that gives love to the living
Becoming love is the source for everlasting love
Death is merely an ending to this life
Though not an end to love
Love is everlasting
Blessed be the day I return to everlasting love
I will tell the source of everlasting love
How grateful I was and still am
That I was chosen for you to love and
God chose you for me to love
How grateful I was and still am
That we loved each other
The greatest love in my life
I will find you again
I will love you again
With everlasting love

Love Awakens

Love may arrive as a gift

Love will nudge you and softly touch your heart

As if gently awakening you from sleep

Destiny and fate hand you something when it is time

They deliver love

Love will whisper in this gift

In its own voice

I am here; can you feel me?

When love awakens, embrace it

It is time to embrace the one who awakened it

Even While Walking

I love him as much when walking by his side
As when we are intimate
To walk next to him, his presence comforts me
We are two but walk as one
I feel his strength
I walk beside him in love
I walk by his side with love
Then he reaches out from his side
For my hand

She is A Queen

She said "have some compassion for me

For what I have been through"

Then she laughed

She laughed with heartache

But also, humor

Why did she get so many crappy hands?

It was just not in the cards for her to win

She knew, and always knew

It was not about winning

It was about how you play the cards that you are dealt

It was being in God's hands and surviving

She prevailed at every attempt at life to take her down

She was a queen in her own right

She conquered the worst that life bestowed on her

All her triumphs over troubles are beneath her

They are her foot stool now

She is a queen with her feet upon it

God's hands put her there

Love Found Me

There is a rare and overpowering love
Unconditional love
It brings ascension to those destined to receive it
A love that illuminates what it awakens
I could say I found this love
Though that would not be true
To believe you found love
Only to find yourself, that is the mystery
I gave my power to love and let it guide me
Love's destination was my soul
How could I know crossing paths with love
Would reveal me
These matters are only for God to know
God uses divine guides on this journey
Fate, destiny, and angels
Led by divine timing
It was my time

Love, Not Age

Like Berries that ripen, and lose their bitterness
They are ready
Everyone thought he mellowed and ripened with age
Though it was not because of age
It was because of her
She was part of his season to change
He had never met any woman like her
And she became his catalyst for change
It was the love she gave him
She did not just offer it
She freely gave it to him
It was her unconditional love
When she met him, she found her love had arrived
At its destination
He changed her also
With challenges and resistance
He changed her for the better
Her love became stronger than ever
Love covers all wrongs
It was painful for him, but he came to the realization
He loved her
It was her, he loved her
It was love that changed him
Not age

Embody Love

There is a rare love, body love
When one's body loves you with their heart and soul
You return their love with body love
You love their body for who they are
You touch their body to connect with their love
You are full of their love
And you are full
When both bodies love each other
You are love, whole love
When you share body love
You embody love

Shed the Nest

Like a companion bird that cannot be mated
The bird may sit on toys or objects and nest
I likened my life to that process
Sitting on my worldly toys
Over giving, overextending
Giving love to objects
To people who do not reciprocate
Putting others ahead of myself
The world's nest is exhausting
Walk off the nest
Live for yourself again
Like a deli or a bakery that offers numbers for service
Always take number one
Put yourself first
Enjoy your new nest of inner peace
And love yourself

Love Gifts

His masculinity stood before me as a gift
Did I cower? No... heaven forbid
I stood as an equal with my femininity
My gift for him
Masculine power standing in the presence of feminine power
I felt his whole presence as he did mine
A preordained meeting of powers
A gift from the highest power
I will accept your masculine love
I will return it in kind with my sacred feminine love
Our love was destined
Soul to soul love is ours

God's Creation

The towering rock pillars reached high into the sky
I sensed and whispered "their years must be billions"
I revered their majesty and heard
"We are sensitive of our age like you
For now, we can say millions"
I found ponderosa tree twigs that lay
Moss covered as beautiful art, beneath the trees
They lay peacefully returning to the earth
Decorating the ground and decaying as they please
Dirt walls stood in magnificent red
Stunning, purely stunning
As I slowly shook my head
The clouds drifted playfully
Atop the mountains that touched the sky
Slipping through the crags and dropping
As though they were tired and once more
They were off to fly

I would say I belong to the earth
When I am in the wild
Though I belong to God and his universe
I am aware that I am his child
What God created, I reverently observe
I will just look at the rock pillars in awe
And not climb, I do not have the nerve
I am grateful for the beauty of the earth
God Almighty created to see
What made it unforgettable was
You were there with me

My Siver Fox

Love will live in many ways
It never leaves your life
It stays
In memories of picking plums
It plays
I fondly cherish our Grainbelt beer days
And your plums turned into beautiful wine
And the lamb you grilled at your shack
Was divine
Your funny glances will live in my mind
Your coffee, with a little whisky to bind
As I look around
I will see you in thin air
And remember you as a silver fox
With a flare
And silver foxes are quite rare
Your memories, I will reverence with care
Light shines on the mystery
When one passes on
They leave parts of themselves
In others
When gone

When Frequency Speaks

I hear his voice
My heart and soul resonate
With the tone of his sound
My heart and soul were unaware
That the tone of a voice
Could cause an awakening
My heart
My soul
Resonate with his frequency
The frequency of his love
And his frequency
God created only for me
All others can only hear his voice

Falling Away

There are times in our lives when
We let people go
Material things lose their attraction
We stop chasing after the feeling of acquiring
Sometimes we must let family go
Sometimes we need to let friends go
Sometimes we leave our jobs
Our homes
When the higher calling calls
Those who have the heart to hear the calling
Answer those calls
We let things go
We leave people behind
We shed
And embrace the falling away
It is a divine calling
To love yourself
To open yourself to new love

The Pedestal

I watched him on his pedestal

Could he truly be everything I saw in him?

My illusion of his being?

That which stands on a pedestal

Is subject to falling off it

One mistake after another

One event after another

His ego out of control

He inched closer to the pedestal edge

He fell off and his pedestal vanished

He suffered some cracks

I looked upon him with compassion

No judgement, mostly not anyway

I offered him forgiveness, not grudges

I will be there for him when he stands again

I cannot help him stand; he must stand on his own

I will be there for him when he stands in his truth

My love will ground him

I found most of my illusion of him was real

He stands on a step stool now

(A nice one)

Finding Me

Just as love found me
When I was not seeking it
I found myself when love made me whole
I am the real version of myself
Now that destiny fated love
Now love fills my soul
Love dissolves the ego
The soul emerges to lead
It cast the light of love before me
To show me
My love is all I need

Self-Respect

Regardless of what the world dumps on you
Your self-respect will see you through
Show the world who you are
With your strength
With your honesty
With your silence
With your love
The world will keep turning
It will keep dumping
Use your self-respect shovel
And make your own way through

Love in Stillness

When words are slow to form to speak
Love will fill the stillness
Love will speak when he takes my hand
To be with him in silence, love is speaking
No words are necessary
Love will communicate
Should he whisper to me
It will be a heart treasure
Possibly, mind candy
My soul is his soul
His love is my love
Being with him in stillness
Is love

Invisible Bridge

When destiny and fate meet at a crossroad
They conspire to bring hearts and souls together
They will join them with an invisible bridge
Heart to heart, soul to soul
It is a bridge you cannot cross
But one worked on from each side
Each heart and soul will build with love
Each side will build structure and stability with love
Building to keep their love safe
They will add respect and devotion towards the other
Their pillars of love will support their bridge
Then love will cross over
One heart and soul to the other
Hearts and souls now bound together
With a bridge only their love can travel

Follow the Path

When you do not know where you are going
Life offers paths with signs
Some clear, some leave you questioning
Follow the path
I could not read the sign
My feet led by my soul, traveled the path
From unconsciousness to consciousness
From falling in love to loving up
And loving myself
On this path I found someone by my side
I found myself in a higher frequency of love
I found myself on this path
I found me, not a destination
And when I did find myself, I saw the sign
I could read it now
It said "You have come to the end of the path"
"You found yourself. You will never be the same"

Bonded in Love Sonnet

You are here, even when you are not here
When I am alone, your heart is in mine
Your presence is ever with me in love
Like a night sky, you are my star, you shine

The love you give fills me with divine peace
So powerful a peace, I feel no fear
And loneliness is only but a word
It has no place even with you not here

Bonded in love, I never feel alone
Bonded in love, my love is now your own

Shadow Work

I touched his shadow, his ego felt my touch
His ego wore a "Do not touch" sign
But when I touched it, he saw me
And I saw him
He tried to find comfort in his shadow
To no avail
It is time to step out of your shadow
Step into the light
See me, I am here
His ego now subjected to a higher calling
His wounded ego let go to let his soul emerge
It was a painful process for him, but he will be a better man
His soul then stepped before the mirror
And we saw each other
We revealed our shared soul to each other
We reflected on each other in love
And found nothing to cast shadows

Feather Messages

Feathered wings fly in the sky
A feather lost may lay nearby
Picking up a feather on the ground
Not just a feather but a message found
It is a sign that you are where you belong
You have been loved and supported all along
What angels cannot voice to a human
They will let the feather say
Angels will loosen the feather on a bird
And guide it to the ground to lay
The universe is in control
God leads and guides your very soul
Often you need just a word
It may come from the feather of a wing
Of a bird

The Old Her

She cannot be found
Her identity went away
Though you may feel her
In the breeze through the trees
In flower petals that lay
In melodious birds singing
In storm clouds on display
She lived her thoughts on any given day
In rock formations
In moss that grows on trees
If she requested of you
She always said please
Where she went, she cannot be found
Though you may feel her
When no one is around
She left a feeling
To pass or to hold
Or feel her inside with her heart of gold
She was but a whisper
Or a thought to entertain
You may feel her presence

In a gentle falling rain
You may think of her in a violent storm
And remember the love she gave you was warm
She was here, but no longer
Her body now her soul
Where ever she went
I know she went whole

Heaven On Earth Sonnet

I awakened to heaven here on earth
When soul to soul you shone your love on me
To walk with new feet upon love's gold path
To have new eyes, my soul does help me see

The gate to heaven opened when we loved
As angels guarded secrets of their plan
To bring two chosen hearts to now unite
To be his only woman, he her man

As angels place their secrets in the heart
Hearts grow with love so deep to never part

My Name

Is my name filling your mind?
Try to remove it, my name will linger
Do you feel my name in your body
Try to stop it
The force is unstoppable
Is my name touching your soul?
Your soul knows what to do
Your soul will whisper to your breath
To say my name
Your body will desire to hold my name
Your soul will confirm, it is love

Soul Control

I quieted my mind from the place of its power
I relieved my mind of its control
I let the rightful ruler now stand
The rightful source, my soul
Soul love is for you; it is not an illusion
It is welcoming you with open doors
Within my soul, is my beating heart
Full of sacred love
It is yours

Holding in Presence

Embrace my body with your body
Hold me with your presence
I will hold you with mine in return
We will exchange body presence
We will exchange soul presence
My body, your body
Your soul, my soul, are one
Our love is only ours
In this presence

The End of the Path

He had trouble looking her in the eye

He knew she could see through him

She saw the man and his soul

He let a glimmer of love shine from his eyes

And he knew it

She saw it and captured it

His ego felt threatened

She was there to trigger his ego

He would need to be the one to threaten it

To make it disappear on the path

The path where he would find his soul

She had been there also

He set her on her path

Now it is his turn

She cannot help him

He needs a kick in the ass to take the path

Life will do the kicking

She will see him at the end of his path

And likewise

He will see her and he will

Look into her eyes with love

Once more

Turtle Crossing

There are times when love arrives slowly
As if you are waiting for a turtle to cross the road
How long will it take to get to its destination?
You learn patience and practice it while you wait
Time is an illusion and it belongs to God
Wait for divine timing to deliver your turtle
Turtles have a built in sense
They know where they need to go
They just need time to get there

No Body

Here I am, my soul does my living
Being no body is a refuge for my soul
Being no body
Not to identify as an occupation
A holder of degrees
Not to feel important for accomplishments
Not to boast of belongings or properties
Not to think I am somebody because of wealth
It is all mind garbage for me
I do not care for the bragging of offspring
I do not care for boasting of children
What they have accomplished
To each his own, but mind garbage for me
The life source I carry allows me to not identify
I am free
I fly with wings of peace
The world can turn without me
How wonderful to have inner peace
How wonderful to be who I am

No body in a somebody world
I am a holder of love
I can share it with whomever I am pleased to
I can love others but will always love myself more
No room for mind garbage
I rest in completion
Not competition

Sacred Fire

He was my vision of sacred fire

He let flames of his love melt to cover me

He poured his protective love over me

He covered me and I became more visible

I was awakened to who I am and for the first time

I saw myself

He exposed and awakened my soul

His fire did not burn me

I could hold it

His liquid fire covered me, all of me

And his liquid fire burst into flames of love in me

To return to the fire it came from

His fire

His love

Just Disappear

When your senses see with clarity
When it is time to move on
Move with swift silence
Move on as though you have disappeared
Be the deer that senses something is not right
And slips swiftly into the trees
Do not leave harsh words that linger
Just disappear
Your absence will be felt
Your absence will stay
While you move on

Reaching

I felt as though I was a baby, a toddler
Who reached her arms out
Reaching out for that feeling
Reaching out for those arms to hold me
For the security
For the comfort
For the love...
It was love

Sunbeam

Some things are hidden from the naked eye
There, captured, but not seen yet
You cannot see it till the time is right
It is like taking a photo
You believe you are looking at something
And when you look to see what you captured
What you were looking at is not there
Something unexpected and far more wonderful was
You caught a sunbeam
A white hot laser beam of sunlight
Not seen by the human eye
But it was there
It is a reminder
You can be looking at something else in your life
There unseen, is love
Shining like a white hot beam of sunlight
It shows up unexpectedly for you
When you finally see it
You also feel it

Trouble Wine

When troubles are ripe and abundant
As berries
Pick a trouble one by one
Crush them and let them ferment
Be sure to add some sweetness to the process
Your troubles will age to perfection
Enjoy sipping your troubles
Taste them
Ruminate on them
Swallow them
You will be a better person for the process
Sipping real wine will also help the process

Okay to Hide

Hide yourself away beautiful woman
Hide yourself away
Do not let him see you for many a day
Let your mind and soul rest free
Hidden is where you need to be
Do not appear in his sight
Chasing him will cause his flight
If you see him, barely speak
The strength in you will make him weak
Missing you gives him desire
His want for you will become dire
His thoughts of you consume his mind
He feels crazy without you
You will find
Stay hidden till he sees the real you
Then he will know what to do
He cannot fight his love for you
It is then
Your hiding days are through

You Know What?

You know what?
At times, I get so pissed off at him
But me, and my unconditional love
I absorb my anger
It is mystical
I turn anger's passion into love
And when I love him
I love him with that passion
That is my forgiveness expressed
I wonder if I really want him to stop
Pissing me off
Forgiveness is powerful

My Epiphany

I had an epiphany
I remembered who I was
I remembered who I am
I am not one to let religion control me
Though I do live for God Almighty
He controls me, not religion
I am not a servant to the world
But to God
I am not a door mat for others to walk over
Or wipe their feet on
I have visions and dreams are a gift
I am not needy or obsessive
I have been mis-judged because of the love I hold
I am not a second class citizen
I am not what the world did to me
In my epiphany I found
I am sovereign
I am a free spirit not to be supressed
Free because God Almighty provides my freedom
I carry love that many cannot fathom

All the love I gave that was rejected
It all returned to me
And I have an overwhelming abundance of love
Now all of my love is mine
I give it all to God and he gives it back to me
For myself
Though I will still give it
When there is a need

His Path

I heard his voice say
"Go ahead, keep working on the path"
I told myself to get a shovel
The path went uphill
It twisted and turned in steepness
I found where the work had stopped
I began digging to lay another stone
I knew it would be a heavy stone to level
So heavy
I will need help with this one
Then I heard a voice of reason speak to me
Stop digging, put the shovel down
This is not your path, it is his
He needs to complete his own path
It is not your place to work on his path
Your path has been completed
You worked hard on your path
Now you can rest
You rest in your peace
He has some heavy soul work to complete on his path
You heard him calling for help, but you cannot help him
You are not even allowed to help put morter between his stones

He must finish his work himself
And when he does
When he does
Both of your paths will become one path
That one, you will travel together

What Were We?

What were we to each other?
Before this life
When we signed soul contracts to find each other
All of this love I carry for you
So much love I have for you
And I cannot stop it
What were we to each other?
That you were the one to awaken my soul
To put me in the hands of the universe
To have angels protecting me
To have angels re-inforcing this love with messages
What a powerful love
That we put ourselves through hell
Without each other for so long, but we did
We knew we would conquer our worldly situations
Victoriously with even more love
It must have been written in our soul contract
How much you love me and how much I love you
I know I loved you or I would not have signed
I could only have agreed to this life for you
It must have been our love for each other
Where is all this love coming from?
I feel you living up to your signature on the contract

She is Open

He talked to her like she was an open window
He felt the breeze and talked while looking towards the window
She was in the breeze
He could feel her
But he could not see her
He looked at her like she was air
She was air
He was breathing her
She thought he could not see her
She was wrong
He did not want to fall in love
But he did
His indifference was a facade
He tried to fight what cannot be fought
Go ahead, look at her
Look at the open window
She is an open window
With a breeze
You can feel it, you feel her
Let her in

He Loves Her

He was eating chips and he told himself
Crying takes a lot out of you
A couple times he choked with emotion
And could not swallow
He was telling himself, he was a jerk to her
She always looked at me with love
And I would not even look at her
All she ever did was love me
I didn't think she would ever leave
I had her wrapped around my little finger, didn't I?
I love her but couldn't let that be part of my life
I pretended I didn't love her
Why do I hurt so bad
I can't keep crying and eating chips
I love her

Wildfire Love

There is love that is not real love

It is a mis-guided and mis-directed feeling

You cling to the feeling

Because you have not had enough experience with love

There is love, true love

You fall in love and you want to love that person

You want the life long commitment and everything that goes with it

The marraige, kids, house and dog

There is sensible love

Maybe you were not in love but you wanted the married life

You wanted the whole package because you felt it was the right thing to do

At the time

Then there is the wildfire love

The love that comes along and passion burns

At times it is a raging passion

You get the flames under control

Maybe you put them out for a while

But you cannot forget the warmth

The heat of the passion

The fire has ignited again, blazing with thoughts

Desiring but also loving with intensity

You love that person with every flame that burns

I will take the wildfire love

I can take the heat

(I'll get the fireplace ready)

Don't Forget Me

Her emotional compass lost its bearing
She began to cry
She had trouble remembering his face
She remembered, but not really
She had visions of him still
Her visions were cloaked in white silk
Sacredly hidden
Painful to have had that love mis-placed
It was taken out of place by destiny
And for love's timing
This love must find its place again
Please destiny, correct love's compass
She does not want to forget him
She loves him
Do not let him forget her

Folding and Freeing

When you carry an unbearable burden
You can either lose yourself or find yourself in it
It could be a separation or a lost love
You can feel like you are hidden
As if you have a sheet of paper in front of you
You have trouble seeing yourself
You can turn that pain into something beautiful
Start letting go by folding the corners of that paper
Let some more of the burden go by making a couple smaller folds
Loving yourself helps the folding
Now fold what is left in half by forgiving
You can make tweaks to the folds
Then you can fold it in half again and again
By loving those near to you and loving yourself even more
It is okay to make a few cuts for what does not serve your creation
Fold that pain away like oragami
Until something beautiful takes shape
Then set it free
Let it go with love
You will see yourself again
You will be more beautiful than you remembered

Struggles and Bears

Struggles can be like bears

You hope you don't run into any

If you meet them you have to figure out how to handle them

You might pray to God to help you

Do not feed your struggles

Or they may keep returning for more

Some struggles may maul you like a bear

Struggles can be dealt with or feared, like bears

You will learn to live in a way where struggles cease

Wisdom will guide you away from struggles

After that, you can still look at bears

It is okay if they scare you

You know how to handle them now

My Hand, Your Heartbeat

As I lay on my bed last night
I placed my hand over my heart
When I did
I could feel and hear your heartbeat in my ears
What a mysterious encounter
I felt every beat of your heart
I could hear the blood pulsing through your arteries
I must have felt it for a whole minute
Were you sending me love? I felt it
I wish I would have counted the heartbeats
Though what I will remember is
Your heart beat as mine
In this good-night visit

The Threshold

Love is the threshold to the universe
God gives his love to us
In time, you learn how to return his love
You learn how to forgive with this love
You learn how to give love
You learn how to receive love
You learn how to love yourself
You live the definition of unconditional love
That is when you cross the threshold to the universe
And you will always be love

Dark Angel

My soul saw him as a dark angel

But an angel none the less

I recognized the darkness but knew

It could not let it hide him

His darkness is the rejection of being loved

He must have perceived himself unworthy of love

What is this encounter from his darkness?

He touched my soul and awakened a powerful light in it

He awakened my power to guide with this light

He knew I was a holder of light

He was from God's light also but he hid in the shadows

Hiding from love

My light will be a guide for him

Though he hid in his darkness, he was not fallen

My soul's light illuminated him

His darkness faded in my love

It is love's light

He will carry it now

We see each other now in love's light

Holding Space

She is holding space for him
She is offering to share her inner self, her soul
It is not a waiting for him space
It is holding space for him in a higher frequency
Should he choose to rise to the occasion
To a space sacred in God
Should he choose to not step into her space
She has not lost
Her space is still her own
Her space is beautiful
It is full of love

The Soul's Scale

I weighed the matter and found it to be unmeasurable

How can you measure weight in the quantum field?

The soul can weigh it

The soul's scale will weigh and balance what can only be seen by the soul

How can you explain what you do not understand?

How can you weigh a heavy heart?

How can you weigh feelings you are tangled in?

Is it matter?

How can you weigh a presence?

When I can feel you endlessly present

When I can feel you and I am alone

How can you weigh the undeniable?

Love

Straight from God

My love comes from the highest source
Straight from God to me
I can radiate my love or keep it for myself
Though I do encounter those who I give it to freely
Where the spirit leads, I follow
God's spirit leads and guides
The spirit knows where there is a need
He brought me to you

Two Bodies, Four Bodies

I love both of your bodies

Your physical body

Your spiritual body

For the physical that embodies the spiritual

And for the spiritual that radiates from your physical

Your heart is the binder for both bodies

I love our bodies together

Two physical bodies to hold each other

Two spiritual bodies to uplift each other

Two hearts joined in love

One soul, we will share one soul

The Laughing Daydream

You stopped by to visit my mind in a daydream

We laughed so hard together

When I told you my thoughts

We started to make love and I considered saying something

To make you slow down, to take your mind off of your drive

I considered saying something motherly to you

Do you remember your mother breast feeding you?

Would that lower your speed?

I wanted our time together to last

When I told you my thoughts you laughed

We both did

We laughed so hard our session took a pause

For a while

Then we loved each other thoroughly

Thanks for your visit

Next time we will laugh in person

Through Me, Through You

He gave it to me through me
He gave me love, God given love
He taught me to give myself love
He wanted me to feel what is is like to be loved by me
God given love will bring you to tears
Overwhelming love you cannot bear the weight of
You balance that with tears and accept it

He gave it to me through me
He gave me strength
Though I felt I was already strong
He showed me I was weak
Through him I grew to be strong
Strong but also silent
What a power in strong silence
What a powerful and most wonderful love
Exchanged between God's Holy Spirit and myself

When God's love whispers to you
It permeates, it goes all the way through
And where ever you go, you pass it to others
It is uncontainable
God given love and you helped me find it
Through me, through you
If our paths would not have crossed
I may never have experienced real love
You brought me to real love and I feel it
I am grateful to you God for your God given love
When you brought him to me
You brought him to me, through you

Mind Games

Was he playing mind games with me?
Was he trying to get me to psychologically submit?
I know a mind game when I see one
I have played a few myself
I will play the game with my own rules
I will act disinterested when he is around
I will walk away in the middle of his stories
I will keep my energy to myself
Soon he will be troubled and will come to me
He will return with questions
Not games
Neither of us will be winners or losers
Just two powers competing a little
On the game board

Self Talk

It is the same feeling you get
When you just sit and visit with a friend
When you do not speak much, you just sit together
And enjoy sitting together
I told myself, we are always together like friends
But we rarely speak
I told myself we could talk about that
Then I told myself...we better not

Time Apart

I have not seen you for a while

Absence and time cannot change my love for you

I remind myself time is an illusion

I do not want to measure the time apart

Even in dreams I see you

In my dreams I understand what you are saying to me

In waking life I am unaware of those words

Sometimes I get mad at you for the hard lessons

You teach me and help my soul grow stronger

At times I do not feel your love, just lessons

One dream I asked you if you could give me just a half cup of love

I said, couldn't you just give me a half cup of love for my recipe

You offered me a handful of wicker balls

When you visit my dreams, do not spare your love

I learn better with love

Every time I am with you again

It is as if no time had come between us

Love erases the voids

And I can remember your love and your words again

Do not forget to give me your love

Celebate Passion

Let my passion be celebate
Do not let it flare for love that I cannot have
Do not let it flare but for the one it is destined for
Let my passion stay with me
Let it stay hidden and I will tend it
Until my chosen love searches for me and finds me
Then I will tend both
Love and passion

When Love
Touches Gratefulness

In the darkness of her bedroom, she shed a few tears

She felt them and touched a few on her heart

For him

Just a few more tears and she felt them

And touched them to her lips

For herself

She touched them to her heart for the heart full of love he gives to her

She touched them to her lips for his lips she was missing

She was grateful for the love he gives her

This is when love touches gratefulness

They were only love tears, not sad tears

When love is wealth to your heart and soul

Love's tears are like diamonds

They will form from the pressure of love

Destined love

Time is irrelevant when love is real

Time apart can make time stand still

Let it stand still when we are together

Not apart

Moving On

A grand vine grew as a pillar
I was on a journey when I encountered the vine
It looked upon me with compassion
The vine reached out to me with tendrils of gold
Touching me enough to keep me near
Though not enough to hold
I studied the vine for a time
Till the vine withered
Till the vine died, I stayed
I will not search for another vine
I will tend what comes my way
I will keep my tendrils to myself, my tendrils of love
I may reach out to touch but not enough to hold
Just as the vine did with me with its tendrils of gold
When the Spirit of God brings another
And whispers to my soul
You are the vine now
Reach out to this one now
Reach out to this one now with all your strength
Wrap your love around this one and grow intertwined now
Two vines intertwined will look for support
They will attach themselves to a pillar
For support
Almighty God the pillar

I Receive, I Give

God whispers words to my conscious
Gentle words for love and support
Firmer for correction and knowledge
He touches me with his presence
He is life for my spiritual body
My lover touches me with words
For love and support
For correction and guidance
With security and support just as God does
He will give all he has for my physical body
My love touches all I encounter
Because of both

Nobody Knows

Where I go, at times I do not even know
God will do the prompting
I will be aware it is time to go
To find the place where I left the path
When you feel your work is done
Return to your path
You can return to your journey
A journey set in place with soul contracts
Sacred planned blueprints created in God's light
I may not get far on the next journey
It may end in a few more steps
I may go so far I will become unrecognizable
I may find myself in another kind of alone
Though never really alone
My angels are ever with me on the path
Should I leave the path, they are ever with me on the journey
Guiding me to my next destined stop
I am no stranger to the path
Just the next destination
Where I go
No one knows, but God

Nobody to the Menches

God gifted me a revelation

I saw myself standing on the side of the path

I was told I was nobody to the menches

I was no body

To be in communion with God's spirit

To have the highest honor

To be no body to the menches

In return, it is a gloriously high honor

To them as well

There is a prophesy to this

They were nobodies to me as well

No bodies, just sacred souls

Nobody can walk the pathless path

No body can walk the pathless path

Only the soul can travel it

I rest in God's sacredness for encountering these souls

May God's presence of love dwell with them for ever more

Parting Music

When love's music grows faint
The volume is so low you barely hear it
So low but it will wake you from your sleep
No more sleep to escape to, I rise
To sit in a chair with the window open and falling rain
I rest with handpan music harmonizing with the rain
To hear two beautiful sounds marry
Soul touchingly beautiful
Soul touchingly sad
To feel my love returning to me unwanted
I fill myself with my love for the loss of yours
I saw the notes being played wrong
Your eyes no longer searched for me
Your vocal chords ignored my ears
You filled the seats around you with others
No room for me
This is the music of parting ways
You played me
But I was aware of the sheet music
The sound of parting ways can be beautiful
When you can feel, hear and see the music
And you know in your heart
God is creating new music for you
Deep beautiful music only for you

He Knows

He knows he hurt her
It takes a big man to admit that to himself
It takes a bigger man to make it right
He felt her love
That is why he could not look in her eyes anymore
If they did happen to lock eyes
He locked up inside
He would just look away, but not fast enough
Just one glance and he could still see her love
She does not deserve this kind of disrespect
And he knows it
She was not just another woman, she was the woman
He knows she will be alright without him
But she is not the one he is worried about
It is time to be the bigger man

Holy Humor

After I had acomplished something great

After an amazing revelation from God

In a celebatory gesture, I slightly lifted both hands to God

Each with a vape, and asked which one

I was going to celebrate and relax with a vape hit

I chose one to inhale only to have a mis-hit and I choked

I choked and coughed

I had been disrespectful to God

I had been disrespectful but he forgave me

Before it even happened

He fills me with so much love and forgiveness

God has a sense of humor

The holiest humor

I was in a great mood and wanted to share my moment with him

He was in a great mood as usual and wanted to forgive me immediately

Before I even asked

He added more love to me

We both had a good chuckle

The self righteous would say I will go to hell for that

God says he loves me unconditionally

He loves me and my sense of humor

And I His

The Fixing

I had been carrying an unexplainable grief
I had carried something far too heavy for my heart and soul
It is not comprehendable to the human mind
To describe the weight of the quantum field
When you can feel the weight of love that exists in another timeline
It can bring an unbearable pain, when you know your love is real
When I know his love is real but I cannot have it
God's timeline operates with God's rules
I wanted to reach out and hold this love but I cannot
I had to reach out to God
I reached far beyond man's love for God's love
I reached out to God for his help and he filled me
His love touched me and the burden disappeared
The pain subsided; it disappeared from my reality
When I was wondering, where is the love I deserve
God gave it to me
It was always him, it was always mine
He touched me with his love in that moment and I became sovereign in it
God's love more powerful than man's
God instilled in my soul, this is not the end of the love I wanted
It is the beginning of the love I needed

God Sufficient

She did not want to call herself self sufficient
She preferred God sufficient
God is sufficient for her
What she looked for in others could not be found
What she looked for was always reflected back to her
What she looked for in God, he gave her, not a mere reflection
What God gave her was real and he gave it abundantly
He gave her love and everything that goes with love
What she sees in herself others cannot see
They cannot see the storms she has been through
Quiet storms and battles she had to fight alone
Pain, betrayal, false friends, rejection, lost love
Things that ripped her to shreds inside
She knew how to hide them
She hid them with God, she would give them all to God
Everything others took from her, God replaced
He gave her love that radiates
His love fills and transforms
She does not need anyone to see her anymore
When you live in God's presence, you no longer seek in others
You have it all with him
God will cause them to see her now
Through him

The Silver Chord

I am bound to God and his universe

I am bound with a silver chord

At times I have put too much friction on the chord

Friction that created silver flames

The flames teach with love

God is the source of this love

He will bring transformation

He will bring you to experience the highest form of love

You will carry it now and share it

Where ever you hear your calling

You will leave all the love you can

Till you hear another calling

If you answer the callings

You will eventually encounter yourself

Should the silver chord part

The greatest love will receive me

Should the silver chord part

Let others catch and hold my silver flames in the parting

See me, and remember me in the flames

And then send them back to God

God's Flames

My heart of gold with silver flames

It will never tarnish

Though someday must go away

Back to my creator who set the burning of the flames

There I will return

The love I carried will never die

It will be added to God's love

To burst and merge with the greatest love

It was your love that caused God's love

To grow with silver flames in my heart

It was the kind of love that could un-do a heart

Though I always knew God's love

It was you who caused my awakening

With a love that does not let go

It is boundless

With an infinate capacity to love

It was your love that burned with mine

To our creator who gave us each other

Our love will ever more be thine

Whoever She Was

Whoever she was, I left her behind
On a path beneath a beautiful tree
Her heart was heavy, too heavy to carry
She now had to part from me
When I left her there
I left her with love
More love than any woman could hold
She reached out
To give me a gift
It was her heart of gold

Whoever he was, I left him behind
On that path beneath a beautiful tree
I left him sitting next to her
To live as a memory
When I left him there
I left him with love
More love than any man could hold
He reached out
To give me a gift
It was his heart of gold

I held his heart, it beat as mine
On that path beneath the beautiful tree
I saw our names engraved in love

In love we would always be
I told him "I cannot have two hearts
I will keep the one that she gave me
You keep yours and give it to her
She is sitting beneath the tree
Though I will keep the names engraved
With love upon my heart
They will be the part of us
Never more to part"

Whoever they were, I left them behind
In love beneath the beautiful tree
I had to make room to carry more love
The love I had for me
When I left them there, I gave them my love
More love than any two people could hold
Their love will live in silver flames
In their gift, my heart of gold

Whoever they were, I left them behind
On a bench beneath a beautiful tree
I left them there
Far behind
Like a whisper
In a memory

The End

My heartfelt gratitude for my cover created by Robbie Jelsma Portfolio 51, Springfield South Dakota.

My heart of gold is especially grateful for MainSpring Publishing

And everyone there who helped me along my path.

www.ingramcontent.com/pod-product-compliance
Lightning Source LLC
Chambersburg PA
CBHW040903120626
46551CB00006B/619